Crosbie

by Iain Gray

79 Main Street, Newtongrange,
Midlothian EH22 4NA
Tel: 0131 344 0414   Fax: 0845 075 6085
E-mail: info@lang-syne.co.uk
www.langsyneshop.co.uk

Design by Dorothy Meikle
Printed by Printwell Ltd
© Lang Syne Publishers Ltd 2021

All rights reserved. No part of this publication may be reproduced, stored or introduced into a retrieval system, or transmitted in any form or by any means (electronic, mechanical, photocopying, recording or otherwise) without the prior written permission of Lang Syne Publishers Ltd.

ISBN 978-1-85217-768-3

Crosbie

MOTTO:
I shall rise again

CREST:
A tree trunk sprouting new branches

TERRITORIES include:
Dumfries and Galloway, Ayrshire

NAME variations include:
Crosby
Crosseby
Crossby
Corsby

Chapter one:

The origins of the clan system

by Rennie McOwan

The original Scottish clans of the Highlands and the great families of the Lowlands and Borders were gatherings of families, relatives, allies and neighbours for mutual protection against rivals or invaders.

Scotland experienced invasion from the Vikings, the Romans and English armies from the south. The Norman invasion of what is now England also had an influence on land-holding in Scotland. Some of these invaders stayed on and in time became 'Scottish'.

The word clan derives from the Gaelic language term 'clann', meaning children, and it was first used many centuries ago as communities were formed around tribal lands in glens and mountain fastnesses.

The format of clans changed over the centuries, but at its best the chief and his family held the land on behalf of all, like trustees, and the ordinary clansmen and women believed they had a blood relationship with the founder of their clan.

There were two way duties and obligations. An inadequate chief could be deposed and replaced by someone of greater ability.

Clan people had an immense pride in race. Their relationship with the chief was like adult children to a father and they had a real dignity.

The concept of clanship is very old and a more feudal notion of authority gradually crept in.

Pictland, for instance, was divided into seven principalities ruled by feudal leaders who were the strongest and most charismatic leaders of their particular groups.

By the sixth century the 'British' kingdoms of Strathclyde, Lothian and Celtic Dalriada (Argyll) had emerged and Scotland, as one nation, began to take shape in the time of King Kenneth MacAlpin.

Some chiefs claimed descent from ancient kings which may not have been accurate in every case.

By the twelfth and thirteenth centuries the clans and families were more strongly brought under the central control of Scottish monarchs.

Lands were awarded and administered more and more under royal favour, yet the power of the area clan chiefs was still very great.

The long wars to ensure Scotland's

independence against the expansionist ideas of English monarchs extended the influence of some clans and reduced the lands of others.

Those who supported Scotland's greatest king, Robert the Bruce, were awarded the territories of the families who had opposed his claim to the Scottish throne.

In the Scottish Borders country – the notorious Debatable Lands – the great families built up a ferocious reputation for providing warlike men accustomed to raiding into England and occasionally fighting one another.

Chiefs had the power to dispense justice and to confiscate lands and clan warfare produced a society where martial virtues – courage, hardiness, tenacity – were greatly admired.

Gradually the relationship between the clans and the Crown became strained as Scottish monarchs became more orientated to life in the Lowlands and, on occasion, towards England.

The Highland clans spoke a different language, Gaelic, whereas the language of Lowland Scotland and the court was Scots and in more modern times, English.

Highlanders dressed differently, had different

customs, and their wild mountain land sometimes seemed almost foreign to people living in the Lowlands.

It must be emphasised that Gaelic culture was very rich and story-telling, poetry, piping, the clarsach (harp) and other music all flourished and were greatly respected.

Highland culture was different from other parts of Scotland but it was not inferior or less sophisticated.

Central Government, whether in London or Edinburgh, sometimes saw the Gaelic clans as a challenge to their authority and some sent expeditions into the Highlands and west to crush the power of the Lords of the Isles.

Nevertheless, when the eighteenth century Jacobite Risings came along the cause of the Stuarts was mainly supported by Highland clans.

The word Jacobite comes from the Latin for James – Jacobus. The Jacobites wanted to restore the exiled Stuarts to the throne of Britain.

The monarchies of Scotland and England became one in 1603 when King James VI of Scotland (1st of England) gained the English throne after Queen Elizabeth died.

The origins of the clan system

The Union of Parliaments of Scotland and England, the Treaty of Union, took place in 1707.

Some Highland clans, of course, and Lowland families opposed the Jacobites and supported the incoming Hanoverians.

After the Jacobite cause finally went down at Culloden in 1746 a kind of ethnic cleansing took place. The power of the chiefs was curtailed. Tartan and the pipes were banned in law.

Many emigrated, some because they wanted to, some because they were evicted by force. In addition, many Highlanders left for the cities of the south to seek work.

Many of the clan lands became home to sheep and deer shooting estates.

But the warlike traditions of the clans and the great Lowland and Border families lived on, with their descendants fighting bravely for freedom in two world wars.

Remember the men from whence you came, says the Gaelic proverb, and to that could be added the role of many heroic women.

The spirit of the clan, of having roots, whether Highland or Lowland, means much to thousands of people.

Meanwhile, many families proudly boast the heraldic device known as a Coat of Arms,.

The central motif of the Coat of Arms would originally have been what was sometimes borne on the shield of a warrior to distinguish himself from others on the battlefield.

Clan warfare produced a society where courage and tenacity were greatly admired

Chapter two:

Bloodlines

A locational name that would have indicated a wayside, or roadside cross, 'Crosbie' and its spelling variants such as 'Crosby' stems from the Old Norse 'kross', meaning 'cross' and 'byr', denoting 'farm.'

By this derivation, the surname Crosby would have described someone who lived near such a cross – one which would have served as a marker for not only a nearby farm but other landscape features and structures such as even a castle.

With such crosses so prevalent across the landscape from earliest times, it is not surprising that 'Crosbie' and its variants are found as place names throughout the British Isles.

In mainland Britain, the name was particularly common in what is now the North Riding of Yorkshire, Lancashire and Cumbria, while north of the border it is mainly associated with Dumfries and Galloway and Ayrshire, although there are also some early mentions of the name in Berwickshire, in the Borders.

It was not until the decades following the Norman Conquest of England in 1066 and subsequent settlement in Scotland of Anglo-Norman families, that the use of surnames such as 'Crosbie' became commonplace.

Previous to this, it was normal for a person to be identified through the use of only a forename, but as population gradually increased and there were many more people with the same forename, surnames were adopted to distinguish one person, or community, from another.

These surnames had a number of sources: some were patronymic, meaning they stem from the forename of one's father – with 'Johnson,' for example, indicating 'son of John', some occupational, such as 'Smith' and 'Miller', and some locational – as was the case with the 'Crosbie' name.

But what were the origins of those in Dumfries and Galloway and Ayrshire who adopted 'Crosbie' and its variants such as 'Crosby' as their surname?

Intriguingly, there are two possible sources – one from an ancient Brittonic, or British, kingdom and the other from those Anglo-Normans who acquired lands and territories north of the border.

Dumfries and Galloway and Ayrshire formed

from the fifth century to approximately 1030 part of the Brittonic Kingdom of Strathclyde, known in the Cumbric tongue as *Teyrnas Ystrad Clut*.

Known by the Welsh as *Hen Ogledd* – the Old North – this vast area embraced northern England and southern Scotland and was also known as *Alt Clut*, from a Brittonic term for the fortress of Dumbarton Rock, its main powerbase.

Having developed during the post-Roman period, the kingdom was originally home to the Brythonic tribe the Damnonii and appears to have become known as 'Strathclyde' – the 'strath' or 'valley' of the (River) Clyde when its centre of power shifted to what is now the Govan area of Glasgow following the sacking of Dumbarton Rock by the Vikings in 870.

Waves of Viking, or Norse invasion and settlement and their inter-breeding with the native Britons and Gaels already settled throughout Dumfries and Galloway and Ayrshire, meant that through time an exotic brew of bloodlines flowed through the veins of those who would come to bear the Crosbie name.

In addition to an infusion of Norse blood through those feared sea invaders the Vikings who raided Scottish shores, the gene pool of the Crosbies was added to by those Normans who fought with William the Conqueror at the battle of Hastings in 1066 and also through Anglo-Normans who had arrived after the conquest.

Records show that among the Norman aristocracy who fought with Duke William was a John de (of) Crosby whose ancestors had held lands in Picardy.

Granted lands at the mouth of the River Mersey, in Lancashire, and naming them 'Crosbie', he had four sons – two of whom, Adam and Thomas, went on to acquire lands in Berwickshire and Annandale, in Dumfries and Galloway.

It was through Adam, owner of the lands in Annandale, that his sons Ivo and Richard and daughter Emphemia famously laid the foundations of an indissoluble bond of kinship with a clan whose name resonates throughout the pages of Scotland's colourful and dramatic history.

This is Clan Bruce, whose most famous son was the great warrior king Robert the Bruce, victor during the First Scottish War of Independence of the battle of Bannockburn in 1314.

Deriving their name from the French 'de Brus', or 'Bruis', in turn derived from their lands of

Brix, the Bruces who settled in Scotland trace descent from Robert de Brus, 1st Lord of Annandale, who did not arrive on British shores for some 40 years after the conquest.

Acquiring lands in England, he was among the many Anglo-Normans who also came to hold Scottish fiefdoms, having settled from south of the border at the invitation of King David I, who had reigned as Prince of Cumbria from 1113 to 1124 and then as Scottish king from 1124 to 1153.

Having been temporarily exiled from Scotland to the court of England's King Henry I, he had become enamoured of Norman customs and culture and, not least, their martial skills and organisational ability and, accordingly, found it to his benefit to have them as allies in his Scottish kingdom.

A companion-in-arms of the king, Robert de Brus, 1st Lord of Annandale, nevertheless took up arms against him in 1138 at the battle of the Standard, near Northallerton, Yorkshire.

This was during an English civil war between the forces of King Stephen I and the Empress Matilda, daughter of the late Henry I and the Scottish king's niece.

Not only was David I's army repelled, but the

Lord of Annandale, had also taken his own son, Robert de Brus, future 2nd Lord of Annandale, who had fought for King Stephen, prisoner.

The bond of kinship between the Crosbies and the Bruces, meanwhile, was cemented when Emphemia, daughter of John de Crosby, married the 2nd Lord of Annandale and her brother Ivo married one of his sisters.

Such close kinship qualifies the Crosbies/Crosbys as a sept, or sub-branch of Clan Bruce.

As such, they are entitled to share in the clan's heritage and traditions that include the right to display its tartan and heraldry of crest and motto – this heraldry recognised by the Lord Lyon King of Arms of Scotland, the final arbiter on all matters heraldic.

In the case of the Crosbies/Crosbys they share the Bruce motto 'We have been' and crest of a lion – while they also have their own proud motto 'I shall rise again' and crest of a tree trunk sprouting new branches.

As kinsfolk of the Bruces, the Crosbies/Crosbys shared in both their glorious fortunes and tragic misfortunes – to the extent that for many centuries their histories were intertwined, particularly during the bitter and bloody Wars of Scottish Independence.

Chapter three:

In freedom's cause

To find the root cause of the Wars of Scottish Independence we have to travel back through the dim mists of time to 1290 when, following the death of the young Margaret, Maid of Norway and heiress to King Alexander III of Scotland, John Balliol became a competitor for the crown.

There were several other competitors, in what became known as the Great Cause, but Balliol's main rival was Robert Bruce, 5th Lord of Annandale and grandfather of the future King Robert the Bruce.

His claim came through the marriage in 1219 of Robert Bruce, 4th Lord of Annandale, to Isobel of Huntingdon, a daughter of Prince David of Scotland, of the Royal House of Dunkeld, 8th Earl of Huntingdon and whose paternal grandfather had been King David I.

Further strengthening the merits of his claim was that Isobel was also a niece of King William I, better known to posterity as William the Lion.

The Scottish nobility had – unwisely, with the benefit of hindsight – asked King Edward I of

England to arbitrate in the matter of the succession and, through his powerful influence, Balliol was pronounced the rightful heir and duly inaugurated as such in November of 1292.

Balliol, born in about 1249, was the son of John, 5th Baron Balliol, Lord of Barnard Castle in England's Co. Durham, and Dervorguilla of Galloway.

But the ambitious and haughty Edward declared himself Lord Paramount of Scotland and Balliol was accordingly treated as a mere vassal, owing fealty to the English monarch.

Deeply rankled by this humiliating state of affairs, a number of Scottish nobles concluded an alliance with France, the Auld Alliance, in July of 1295, and Edward's response was to invade the northern kingdom.

As his forces wreaked fire and havoc across Scotland, Balliol was forced to abdicate in July of the following year and, on Edward's orders, the proud arms of Scotland were formally torn from his tunic – giving the hapless Balliol the nickname of 'Toom Tabard', or 'Empty Coat.'

Imprisoned for a time in the Tower of London, he was later allowed to retire to his French estates in Picardy, where he died in 1314.

The Scots rose in revolt against the imperialist designs of Edward in July of 1296 but, known as 'the Hammer of the Scots', he brought the entire nation under his subjugation little less than a month later, garrisoning strategic locations throughout the length and breadth of the nation, and demanding the signing of a humiliating treaty of fealty.

Signed – reluctantly it has to be stressed – at Berwick by 1,500 Scottish earls, bishops and burgesses, the parchment is known as the *Ragman Roll* because of the profusion of ribbons that dangle from the seals of the signatories – among whom was the future King Robert the Bruce.

But subjugation under the iron fist of English occupation did not sit well with the proud Scots, and the great patriot William Wallace raised the banner of revolt in May of 1297.

A charismatic leader and an expert in the tactics of guerrilla warfare, he and his hardened band of freedom fighters set Scotland aflame – boosting the morale of their fellow countrymen as they inflicted a stunning series of defeats on the English garrisons.

This culminated in the liberation of practically all of Scotland following the battle of Stirling Bridge, on September 11, 1297.

But, defeated at the battle of Falkirk on July 22, 1298, after earlier being appointed Guardian of Scotland, Wallace was eventually betrayed and captured seven years later, and brutally executed in London as a 'traitor' on August 23, 1305.

His execution only served to further inflame Scottish passions, and the cause of the nation's freedom was taken up again, this time under the inspired leadership of Bruce, who had been enthroned as king at Scone in March of 1306.

Only a month, earlier, however, he had incurred the wrath of the Comyns for the slaying in the Greyfriars Church in Dumfries of his bitter rival and fellow Guardian of Scotland John Comyn, known as the 'Red Comyn' in contrast to his father John Comyn II, who had been known as the Black Comyn.

The exact circumstances surrounding the killing of the Red Comyn remain a mystery, but legend holds he and Bruce had become involved in a heated argument over the terms of a pact the pair are said to have made – culminating in Bruce stabbing him before the high altar.

Shocked by his action, Bruce is said to have staggered out of the church and informed a small band of his waiting supporters – including Robert Crossbi, a descendant of the 12th century John de Crosby – that he 'thought' he had killed Comyn.

His loyal followers Sir Robert Fleming and Roger Kirkpatrick are reputed to have said: "You doubt! I mak siccar!" – "I make sure!" – then they rushed in and Fleming later exited bearing Comyn's head and exclaiming: "Let the deed shaw (show)".

It was for the slaying of the Red Comyn, a deed that sent shockwaves throughout Europe, that Bruce was excommunicated by Pope Clement V.

Over the next six years, Bruce experienced defeats that included the battle of Methven on June 19, 1306 and the battle of Dalrigh, near Tyndrum, Perthshire on August 1 of that year.

But despite these initial defeats and other setbacks, he achieved a stunning series of victories over the occupying English forces that include the battle of Glen Trool, fought on his home turf of the Southern Uplands of Galloway in April of 1307 and the battle of Loudoun Hill, in Ayrshire, the following month.

This latter battle, featured in the 2018 historical action film *Outlaw King*, with actor Chris Pine in the role of Bruce, was a particularly significant victory laying as it did the groundwork for tactics that would be successfully employed in his decisive victory over King Edward II at the battle of Bannockburn in 1314.

This was when a 20,000-strong English army was defeated by a Scots army less than half this strength.

Ironically, it was through a misguided sense of chivalry that the battle occurred in the first place.

By midsummer of 1313 the mighty fortress of Stirling Castle was occupied by an English garrison under the command of Sir Philip Mowbray.

Bruce's brother Edward agreed to a pledge by Mowbray that if the castle was not relieved through battle by midsummer of the following year, then he would surrender.

This made battle inevitable, and by June 23 of 1314 the two armies faced each other at Bannockburn, in sight of the castle.

It was on this day that Bruce slew the English knight Sir Henry de Bohun in single combat, but the battle proper was not fought until the following day, shortly after the rise of the midsummer sun.

The English cavalry launched a desperate but futile charge on the densely packed ranks of Scottish spearmen known as schiltrons, and then found themselves cunningly 'funnelled' by Bruce onto a narrow section of boggy land bordered by the Pelstream and Bannock burns.

Unable to manoeuver, they were slaughtered in their hundreds, while many more including infantry were drowned in the burns as they attempted to flee.

By the time the sun had sank slowly in the west the English army had been totally routed, with Edward II only narrowly managing to make his escape from the carnage of the battlefield.

But, among the Scots dead were no fewer than five of the seven sons of Robert Crossbi, who had been present at the slaying of the Red Comyn eight years earlier.

Rather bizarrely, one of these sons was Adam Crossbi – said to have been slain by his father for fighting on the side of the English.

One of his surviving sons, Robert Crossbi, fought under Bruce's younger brother Edward Bruce in his Irish campaign of 1315 to 1318.

This was after Bruce had despatched envoys to the royal house of the O'Neills of Ulster and other Irish chieftains in the early months of 1315, appealing to their shared Celtic identity in the face of English oppression.

The O'Neill king of Ulster responded by saying he was willing to renounce his right to the High Kingship in favour of Edward.

Accordingly, in May of 1315, Edward Bruce sailed from the Scottish west coast port of Ayr in a fleet of 300 galleys carrying 6,000 veteran soldiers including Robert Crossbi.

Landing at Larne, near Carrickfergus, he quickly rallied fellow Celtic support in his daring bid to defeat the occupying Anglo-Irish forces that owed allegiance to Edward II, and among his allies were not only the O'Neills, but also the McCarthys.

Bruce gained a series of stunning victories in the initial months of his campaign, including the capture of both Carrickfergus and Dundalk, and was inaugurated as the High King of Ireland on May 2, 1316.

But the Anglo-Irish forces rallied shortly after his inauguration, and the next two years were marked by a bloody series of advances and reversals for his forces until, in October of 1318, he was killed in battle at Faughart, near Dundalk.

In a later century, some bearers of the Crosbie/Crosby name were among those Scots Protestants settled or 'planted' on Irish land at the expense of native Irish deemed rebellious by the English Crown.

This policy of 'plantation' had started during the reign from 1491 to 1547 of Henry VIII, whose Reformation effectively outlawed the established Roman Catholic faith in his dominions.

The settlement continued throughout the reigns of Queen Elizabeth I, King James I (James VI of Scotland) and King Charles I, exploding in an insurrection in 1641 that was subsequently quelled.

Uprisings against English rule broke out in the Irish Rebellion of 1798, known in Irish-Gaelic as *Éirí Amach* 1798 and which had been organised by the republican revolutionary group the United Irishmen.

Despite support from a French army that landed in Co. Mayo, the rebellion was crushed, leaving a death toll estimated at between 10,000 and 30,000.

Among its victims was the United Irishman Sir Edward Crosbie, who had succeeded to his father's baronetcy in 1773, when aged eighteen, as 5th Baronet Crosbie of Maryborough in Queen's County.

Having studied at Trinity College, Dublin

and called to the bar, he joined the United Irishmen and was executed for treason on June 5, 1798 for his role in the rebellion – although some evidence suggests he may have been the victim of a miscarriage of justice.

Chapter four:

On the world stage

Bearers of the Crosbie name and its popular spelling variant Crosby have achieved international recognition through a wide and colourful range of endeavours and pursuits.

Known for her role from 1990 to 2000 in the BBC television sitcom *One Foot in the Grave*, **Annette Crosbie** is the award-winning Scottish actress born in 1934 in Gorebridge, Midlothian.

Despite her parents' initial disapproval of her becoming an actress, she pursued her ambition by studying at the Bristol Old Vic Theatre School and went on to perform in a number of notable television and film productions.

These include *The Six Wives of Henry VIII*, which won her the 1971 BAFTA TV Award for Best Actress and also for the 1976 *Edward the Seventh*.

Also nominated for the BAFTA Award for Best Actress in a Supporting Role for the 1976 *The Slipper and the Rose*, other film credits include the 2003 *Calendar Girls* and, from 2014, *Into the Woods*.

In addition to *One Foot in the Grave*, in

which she played Margaret, the long-suffering wife of Victor Meldrew, played by fellow Scots actor Richard Wilson, other television credits include a revival of A.J. Cronin's *Dr Finlay* and the 1997 to 2001 series *An Unsuitable Job for a Woman*.

A campaigner for greyhound welfare and adopted president of the League Against Cruel Sports in 2003, through her marriage to Michael Griffiths she is the mother of the English actress **Selina Griffiths**.

Born in 1969 and known for her role of Pauline Maltby in the sitcom *Benidorm*, her other television credits include the sitcoms *Come Fly With Me* and *Not Going Out*.

Born in 1903 in Tacoma, Washington, but moving with his family when aged three to Spokane, Harry Lillis Crosby Jr. was the legendary American entertainer better known as **Bing Crosby**.

The recipient of three stars on the Hollywood Walk of Fame – for motion pictures, radio and audio recording – he was the fourth of seven children.

Of Irish roots through his mother and Scottish through his father, he once explained how his nickname "Bing" came about through a favourite childhood pastime playing 'Cops and Robbers' armed with wooden six-shooters.

While shooting his 'victims', he would imitate the sound of gunfire by loudly exclaiming: "Bing! Bing! Bing!"

The nickname stuck, and it was as Bing Crosby he achieved international adulation and acclaim as a singer, comedian and actor – with a poll of fellow-Americans in 1948 declaring him "the most admired man alive."

Recipient in 1963 of the first Grammy Global Achievement Award, as a singer or 'crooner' as he was affectionately known, his many hits include the Irving Berlin composition *White Christmas*, first introduced on a Christmas radio broadcast in 1941 and, recorded a few months later, then featured in his 1942 film *Holiday Inn*.

In addition to *White Christmas*, three more of his top hits have been included in the Grammy Hall of Fame – the 1936 *Pennies from Heaven* and, both from 1944, *Swinging on a Star* and *Don't Fence Me In*.

Interested in audio and film technology, Crosby invested a substantial sum in the California-based electronics company Ampex, pioneering reel-to-reel recording techniques and also becoming the first performer to pre-record his radio shows.

Also having helped to finance the development

of videotape, he was a racehorse breeder and co-owner of the Pittsburgh Pirates baseball team.

As an actor, he was the recipient of an Academy Award for Best Actor for his role of Father Chuck O'Malley in the 1944 *Going My Way* and, reprising the role a year later in *The Bells of St Mary's*, nominated in the category.

Also on the silver screen, he starred between 1940 and 1962 with Bob Hope and Dorothy Lamour in the series of *The Road to...* musical comedies including the 1940 *The Road to Singapore*, the 1942 *The Road to Morocco* and, from 1962, *The Road to Hong Kong*.

Having influenced the singing style of many other top performers including Frank Sinatra, Perry Como, Dick Haymes and Dean Martin, he died in 1977.

On Scottish shores and in the world of contemporary music, Gerard Crosbie is the singer, songwriter and acoustic guitarist better known by his stage name **Gerry Cinnamon**. Born in 1984 in the Castlemilk district of Glasgow, it was after performing a solo gig that he teamed up with fellow Glaswegian Chris Marshall, who took on the role of arranger and producer of his songs.

Along with Lori Duncan, Gav Hunter and

Dave Bass, he formed the band The Cinnamons – later adopting the name for his subsequent successful career as a solo artist.

First coming to attention through social media and word of mouth, his popular singles include *Hope Over Fear*, *Belter*, *Sun Queen* and *The Bonny*.

The subject of the 2019 documentary *David Crosby: Remember My Name*, **David Crosby** is the American singer, songwriter and musician born in 1941 in Los Angeles.

A founder member in 1964 of the Bob Dylan backing-band the Byrds, enjoying hits including *Mr Tambourine Man*, in 1968, along with Stephen Stills and Graham Nash, he formed Crosby, Stills and Nash (CSN) and later, with the addition of Neil Young, Crosby, Stills, Nash and Young (CSNY), with hit albums including *Déjà Vu*.

A two-time inductee of the Rock and Roll Hall of Fame, for his work with the Byrds and CSN, he traces a descent through his father from the Van Rensselaer family, prominent in American political and business affairs throughout the seventeenth, eighteenth and nineteenth centuries and from whom Herman Melville, author of *Moby Dick*, also traced a descent.

His father was the award-winning cinematographer **Floyd Crosby**, born in 1899 in West Philadelphia; winner of the 1931 Academy Award for Best Cinematography for *Tabu: A Story of the South Seas*, and a Golden Globe Award for his work on the 1952 *High Noon*, he died in 1985.

Bearers of the Crosbie name have also excelled in the highly creative world of art.

Born to Scottish parents in Hankow, China in 1915 and returning to Scotland with his family when aged eleven, **William ("Bill") Crosbie** was the noted artist who studied at Glasgow School of Art from 1932 to 1934 and later in Paris. Setting up his studio in Glasgow, he became particularly renowned for his mural paintings, many of which were commissioned by the eminent architects Jack Coia and Basil Spence.

He died in 1999, while his work is now held not only in private collections but also in a number of Scottish galleries and museums, the British Museum and the Royal Collection.

One particularly colourful and daredevil bearer of the Crosbie name was **Richard Crosby**, proudly hailed by his fellow country folk as "The first Irishman to fly" and the brother of the ill-fated Sir Edmund Crosbie, 5th Baronet, referred to in the previous chapter.

Born in 1755, he was fascinated with the challenge of flight and experimented with a number of hydrogen-filled balloons – one of which, 'manned' by a bemused cat, had to be rescued by a passing ship after being spotted over the west of Scotland before descending near the Isle of Man.

It was two years after the first manned balloon flight by the French Montgolfier Brothers that Crosbie, on January 19, 1785, took to the heavens in a hydrogen-filled balloon from Ranelagh, on the south side of Dublin and witnessed by an excited crowd of more than 35,000.

His intention was to cross the Irish Sea in his grandly named Aeronautic Chariot, dressed as he was in 'a robe of oiled silk, lined with white fur, his waistcoat and breeches in one, of white satin quilted, and morocco boots, and a Montero cap of leopard skin.'

The descent of darkness thwarted his attempt to cross the Irish Sea but, landing safely at Clontarf, on the north side of Dublin instead, he had nevertheless indeed qualified as the first Irishman to fly.

He died in 1824, while his flight is commemorated through *The Artist* statue in Ranelagh Gardens.